Jan 2013

P T S D

My Story, Please Listen!

POST TRAUMATIC STRESS DISORDER

An Autobiography by

Curtis Butler III

authorHOUSE®

AuthorHouse™
1663 Liberty Drive
Bloomington, IN 47403
www.authorhouse.com
Phone: 1-800-839-8640

POST TRAUMATIC STRESS DISORDER

Post Traumatic Stress Disorder (PTSD) is about the
silent trauma from which our soldiers are suffering
and the author's own experience.

First published by AuthorHouse 5/21/2010

ISBN: 978-1-4520-2896-5 (e)
ISBN: 978-1-4520-2895-8 (sc)

Library of Congress Control Number: 2010907418

Printed in the United States of America
Bloomington, Indiana

This book is printed on acid-free paper.

PREFACE

This book was written by a Soldier with Post Traumatic Stress Disorder (PTSD) dealing with his daily struggles with this disorder or in his words "trying to rid the dancing devils in my head". To capture the author's essence of his thoughts and statements only minor editing has been performed.

Flashbacks, intrusive emotions, bad memories, nightmares, explosive outburst and irritability are symptoms of PTSD.

The author chronicles his life from childhood to the present with emphasis on his experience in the service to his country and the injustices he saw during his service career.

This autobiography exposes the realism of the government's inability to address the needs of countless members of our Armed Forces that experienced the atrocities of the present conflict in Iraq and Afghanistan, the need to fight Veteran's homelessness and above all getting the right medical treatment for those who suffer from this very traumatic disease.

Author Curtis Butler III

Guard Duty in Baghdad

DEDICATION

To my fellow Soldiers:

There is a dancing devil in our heads
That raged emotion both of rage and fear

And where our frown of hated darkly fell
Hope, withering, fled and mercy sighed farewell.

Longview

ACKNOWLEDGEMENTS

To my Dad,

I dedicate Post Traumatic Stress Disorder "My Story, Please Listen" to my Dad Curtis Butler Junior. Thank You for telling me to keep fighting. Love you Dad.

To my grandparents in Heaven, I dedicate "Curtis Butler III - Like Him or Love Him".

To my grandparents in heaven, Mr. and Mrs. Curtis Butler Senior,

So many words cannot describe the way I feel about you, my two loving grandparents. You bent over backwards when you did not have the means to do so. Your strength was as strong as one hundred men. You did things for the family that amazed me in many ways. I cry sometimes because I want to be as strong as you were and one day take care of my family as you did ours. I thank God for blessing me with you.

Thank You Granddad and Grandma, 'til we meet again.

Thank you to my friend Lewis Woodard, my dentist Doctor George Bilbro and his wonderful staff.

Curtis Butler III

My outfit *Old Ironsides*

TABLE OF CONTENTS

Curtis Butler III standing tall, looking good at
LaGuardia Airport Queens New York

CHAPTER ONE
Closing the Revolving Doors

I grew up around many different women that my Dad passed me off too and told me she was my Mother. Nevertheless, I knew deep down inside that these women were not my Mother. I watched my Dad do things to women that I would not dare do and heard him say. I always wondered why the women stayed around for the abuse that they encountered in the hands of my Dad. For many years, I resented my Dad for what he put my brother and sisters through. Too this day, my sisters do not speak to or have contact with my Dad. My brother speaks to my Dad even though he was treated badly also.

I just recently started speaking to my Dad. I had wanted to take him out for all of the pain and hurt he has put us through. I had family that stuck by me, and counselors and doctors who told me to channel my thought process to being a positive role model for my kids. I hated myself because I was becoming my Dad by not taking care of my kids and by being a free spirit like he was. I was running the streets like a wild animal and chasing any skirt who would give me the time of day.

My Dad kept us from one another growing up, so we missed out on our childhood. He would tell the women he messed with that he only had a son which was me. The things my Dad did have affected us mentally, physically and emotionally. I did not know who my Mom was until I was nineteen years old. To this day, we do not have a relationship, but I still love her because she had me. I do not think my sisters will ever forgive him and I pray that my sisters can put it into their hearts to forgive as I did.

What I was lacking was a Mother figure, a woman to teach me how to love and respect women and others, especially my wife. I look to my aunts as my heroes because they did their best to make me the man that I am today. I do not blame my aunts for my relapse; I have had a lot of trauma in life from a divorce, breakups, losing a fiancé and my stepdaughter, losing my daughters, and losing Soldiers in the War on Terrorism.

Now, I am taking the advice I need from my family and doctor/ counselors to forgive and to live my life differently from my Dad. Therefore, I called my daughters and apologized for treating them the same way my Dad did his kids and my daughters forgave me. I called my Dad and told him that I miss speaking with him. He responded, "Same here". As we were getting ready to hand up, he said, "I love you" and I said, "I love you too". That shit really felt good. We continued to speak and text one another. I feel now that the healing has begun and there is no need to beat up my Dad anymore.

My Dad and I have the same issues and we both are disabled veterans, so he was the one who told me not to give up fighting for my compensation. I have been listening and fighting for what is right and things are looking better. No matter what your parents do or say to you, God said we must obey our parents so that our days on earth will be longer. By me doing the right things, many good things have happened to me. When I look back at my past, it was a test that God gave me that I had been failing for years. I am a much better person now than I was then. Some people take anger to their graves. I do not want to get to Heaven and for GOD to ask me "How can you love me, if you have never seen me and don't love your neighbor that you see every day?" Come back when you grow up.

People have to learn how to love themselves before they start to love anyone else. This is part of the healing process for us as human beings and we need to understand this. Life is precious; Life is a gift that we do not appreciate. Every day that we do not forgive a person for wrong doing, it will not stop this revolving door or cycle. We cause harm to ourselves and the people around us.

PFC Curtis Butler III
Baghdad 2003—2005

2

CHAPTER TWO
Homeless Veterans

A third of America's homeless population has served our country in the Armed Forces and we have approximately 200,000 veterans' male and females, on any given night during the year are experiencing homelessness in America. Many other veterans are considered close to becoming homeless, due to misfortunes in life, poverty level and don't have any support from family and friends.

I lost my family due to drugs and almost became homeless and suicidal. I am a Veteran of two wars, currently pursuing a Bachelor's Degree in Business and Accounting with a grade point average of 3.56. I am an ex-military Soldier struggling with Post Traumatic Stress Disorder, and have not let this disease stop me from living a fruitful life. I have been on interviews with KFOX news numerous times, El Paso Times, Channel 26 and 1150 AM radio and 1340 AM radio. Speaking about the Veterans Administration, our disabled Veterans and Homeless Veterans who are not receiving their benefits and disabilities services that are rightfully theirs due to not having medical records or the problem not diagnosed in their medical records. "Butler for Vets" with the help of our citizens here in El Paso, Texas, we would house all homeless veterans in a long term shelter, in which we will have accountability of all veterans. Take them to job interviews and once they are employed, we will help them get housing. In close alliance with the Vet Center of El Paso, VA, GI Forum, Workforce Center, SBA, VSBA, VFW and DAVE have the ability to serve our clients effectively. This way our economy picks up and the veterans pay taxes, as they become productive members of society. Having experienced all the challenges our veterans face, we can implement the needed changes in their situations.

Mission Statement:

To be a benchmark organization that specializes through its community partnerships in providing the highest quality services to all military members. No Soldier will wait thirty years to receive his or her benefits. It is time to close the revolving doors. Wake up America, we are falling behind.

The Department of Veterans Affairs states the number of homeless males and females who have served in Vietnam is at a much higher number of service people who died during the war and a small amount of Desert Storm Veterans are appearing homeless in today's society. Many of our veterans have served in a combat zone and suffer from Post Traumatic Stress Disorder (PTSD). The Veterans Affairs did a study and said there is no service connected disabilities between military service, or exposure to combat being the reason for homelessness with our veterans.

They say the lack of family and friends support and personal character of the Soldier rather than military service are the cause of homelessness. I totally disagree. Most homeless veterans are males, only about three percent are women. The vast majority are single and most come from poor disadvantaged background. However, most homeless veterans are older and more educated than non veterans. Forty-five percent of the population of homeless veterans males suffer from mental illness and more than seventy percent suffer from alcohol or other drug abuse problem.

Everyone is at fault. This is the reason why we cannot be treated for these symptoms; because of the mentality and the words of a physician who is book smart and who has never been in a war zone. These are the types of fallacies that our government has us to believe "if it's not broke don't fix it". Welcome home heroes, good job.

That is a slap in the face, to call us heroes and then deny us benefits. I wonder if the service men and women working at the White House go through what we go through. Large amounts of veterans who are homeless are males and roughly three percent are women. The majority is single and come mostly from poor disadvantaged backgrounds. Most homeless veterans are older and more educated than non veterans. Forty-five percent or more of the population of homeless veterans suffers from mental illness and more than seventy five percent suffer from alcohol or other drug abuse problems. About sixty percent are African American or Hispanic, WOW! We do not need a change we need right now.

About 1988, a group of Vietnam Veterans from San Diego formed the first Stand Down. Since then, this has been an effective tool to reach out to homeless veterans, reaching over 200,000 veterans and their family members during 1994-2000.

During peacetime, Stand Down gives homeless veterans one to three days of safety and security for which they get food, shelter, assistance, health care and links to other programs.

The Veterans Industries is a work therapy/transitional residence program which help disadvantaged at risk and homeless veterans live in a supervised group community. While working, they receive $732.00 a month for 33 hours of work per week. The Veteran pays $186.00 a month for the maintenance of their residency. The veterans reside at this place for up to 174 days. During that stay the veterans learn new job skills and regain a sense of self-esteem and self worth.

The Community Homelessness Assessment, Local Education and Networking Groups (CHALENG) are other programs to assist veterans through local, state and federal agencies to assess needs of homeless veterans. There programs have local directories that contain community resources that homeless veterans can refer to.

The Domiciliary Care for Homeless Veterans (DCHV) is a service that provides bio-psychosocial treatment and rehabilitation for our homeless veterans. This program provides treatment for veterans with health problems. The program lasts four months and assists 5,000 homeless veterans a year. DCHV has vocational counseling and rehabilitation and post-discharge community support. The Drop-In Care Center is a program that allows homeless veterans a daytime sanctuary

where they can wash their clothes, clean up, and participate in therapeutic and rehabilitative activities.

When Soldiers transition out of the military, it is not an easy task, you have to take a final medical test, take classes in working in the civilian sector and wait for our disability checks. Soldiers like me have disabilities and the Veteran Administrators put Soldiers through a lot of red tape. What I have noticed about the Veterans Administration is that they like to shift the responsibility or blame in order to make themselves look like they are doing their best to assist us. Not all VA personnel do this. We have people working to assist in the care of our Veterans and the homeless, and we appreciate this act of kindness. I wish and pray that all VA representatives do the same. Let us stop killing our history, which are our veterans from past and present. It is time to close the revolving door. VA needs to hire physicians who have been to the war zone and lived and worked in those hospitals that run like a well tuned engine, hire Soldiers who could give you input and help other Soldiers and family members that have everyday stress in their lives. Stop telling Veterans they cannot say certain things when speaking to their physicians, if we do not let them know what is wrong with us, how can you assist or treat us properly. Remember, we have been in the war zone for many months and will live under that stress for the rest of our lives.

CHAPTER THREE
PTSD does not have to ruin or run your life

MANAGING BUSINESS ETHICS

I will give you a brief synopsis of three businesses which have ethical issues that are hurting our community and the world as we see it. I will also explain what my definition of business ethics is and if they apply. First will be a discussion on the Veterans Administration and how they deal with veterans with Post Traumatic Stress Disorder, our local government on dealing with Post Traumatic Stress Disorder, our local government on dealing with Post Traumatic Stress Disorder and the last issue will be the past and present Presidents on the treatment of our disabled veterans. You will understand when I put this puzzle together, you will find the fallacies and that the business ethics only works for some and not all.

In my humble opinion, the inattention by our government; the most powerful and plentiful government in the world is to blame for the countless veterans roaming the streets of our nation.

Business Ethics and my understanding of this work is the behavior or standards of a company of GOVERNMENT who agrees to obey policies accordingly while dealing daily with the business world. This agreement applies not only to how business is done in the world, but also on a one to one dealing with our Soldiers and veterans. Our government is one of many businesses that have a bad reputation, businesses like this are all about making money and they tend to forget who put them in office.

BUSINESS ETHICS OF THE VETERANS ADMINISTRATION

Our government is supposed to help out the hero veterans who fought for the FREEDOM of the American citizens. They lie and have been practicing these fallacies for many years and still do. All you have to do is go online and look up VAWatchdog.org.

Medical Mistreatment: Gross Betrayal of Veterans Nobody is Responsible; these are just some of the websites you can go to: www.veteransforcommonsense.com

The VA denies veterans benefits because it's costly to the taxpayers, isn't that a kick in the teeth? The VA, whether they send you a letter in the mail or not for specialized tests, can deny your benefits and get away with this daily. The VA gives you medicine and tells you if you do not continue to take the medicines and get refills they will deny your benefits. I have been on so many medicines from the VA, some days I look high as a kite.

Our VA is one of the worst facilities around and I am surprised that they are still in business. In the Executives Office on the fourth floor in the VA building are a bunch of high paid idiots that lie to the news media and to me, in order to make themselves look good. If that is our tax money working at its best; well, I hope we never see the worst. You can also go to www.ptsdmystorypleaselisten, this is my Face Book and read about the disturbing things the VA put their veterans through and ask yourself if all veterans from past to present are being treated fairly.

BUSINESS ETHICS IN EL PASO GOVERNMENT DEALING WITH POST TRAUMATIC STERSS DISORDER

When it comes to our representative, some not all, fall short when it comes to our veterans that come back home with Post Traumatic Stress Disorder. We have conferences and book readings on this subject matter and they are invited; do they show? No, they do not because they do not have an interest all. I have emailed and called certain representative here in El Paso, no response. But news about a man kissing another man in a restaurant or the closing of an adult club and the representatives run to their aid. Are we that frivolous?

www.DrPhilLevequeSalem-News.com

Why can't the military Soldiers and families receive this treatment when they are faced with issues returning home and why when a Soldier is back home and they do something unlawful, no matter how minor, they want to lock them up and throw away the key. The reason why is because they are high paid and they want to make themselves look good instead of look right. (Dr. Phil Leveque Salem-News.com)

Wake up America, we're falling behind. Most of these representatives want to know what you can do for them and what they can do for you. Half of us do not know our representatives until you see them on the billboards saying re-elect me to office. At what cost are we selling ourselves short?

www.veteransforcommonsense.com

BUSINESS ETHICS OF PAST AND PRESENT PRESIDENTS ON THE TREATMENT OF OUR DISABLED VETERANS

To the last two Presidents, the American people would like to know why you lied to the people you were supposed to help protect; there were no weapons of mass destruction. How do you sleep at night knowing you are receiving blood money from Soldiers losing their lives because of your business ethics, lies and deceit? We should have tried you in court and hold you and staff accountable for the heinous crimes you have committed on U.S. soil.

If this was an ordinary citizen, they would be facing life in prison. We taxpaying citizens need to hold all our government officials accountable for all acts while in office and if they do not honor their position, they should be held accountable to the offense. Remember America, when you do not follow company of business ethics, you may be terminated.

Mr. President, what are you and your staff doing to help our Soldiers and their family members to cope with Post Traumatic Stress Disorder? All we hear is blah, blah, blah. We see taxpayer's money going everywhere else except to the right people, the people who voted for you. Do you know Louisiana is still not rebuilt yet? Hell, it looks like Baghdad. What about your people Mr. President, stop worrying about what the world is thinking and take care of your family which is the United States. I understand disasters happen and my prayers go out to everyone; but we have had disasters for over forty years Sir. You said it is time for a change and I see you doing the same things every other President is doing, passing the buck.

Why haven't any Presidents signed a Bill to help stop homelessness of our veterans and civilian counterparts? We pass Bills for everything except that, why? I hold you and your whole staff accountable for your actions. Mr. President, if your freedom is not worth a Bill pass for the men and women fighting to keep America FREE, maybe you need to step down and put a Soldier in your position.

If all veterans and their dependents should start shopping on base here in Texas and at all other installations in the United States, what do you think will happen? Our government would probably use better business ethics. It would be cheaper to make sure our veterans, after they fought a hard fought war, are treated properly and receive their entitled benefits.

This goes to all of our Presidents and staff living off the hog of all of the disasters we have had, like Pearl Harbor, the World Trade Center and other tragedies. What county assisted us? Every time we go to war with a county, we help them rebuild. Again, I ask, who helps us rebuild? It seems like we pay taxes so that other countries can benefit from.

From my experience and what I can see in the streets of our city, the following quote truly applies.

"We're going to be having a tsunami of homeless veterans eventually, because the mental health toll from this war is enormous". – Daniel Tooth, Director of Veterans Affairs, Lancaster County, PA.

The Homeless Veterans deserves our help. In Conclusion, let me comment on the state of our leaders.

As you can tell, the apple does not fall far from the tree when it comes to business ethics in the government. If the leaders of our country have bad business ethics, why can't I?

That's why businesses are failing because there is no pride: it's all about what I can get and how fast can I get it without getting caught. If I get caught, I will keep lying or pass the blame to the next President elect.

And the fight goes on.

CHAPTER FOUR
Wake up America, We're falling behind

The Veterans Business Association is a nonprofit organization that helps Veterans start new business ventures in partnership with the Veterans Business Resource Center. This project was developed to empower U.S. Armed Forces Veterans, Active Military Service members, National Guard and Reservists and their families by helping them solve challenges they face after being discharged from the U.S. Armed Forces.

I believe that the true measure of society is its ability to acknowledge and reward the contributions of all its members, especially those who contribute something as important as putting their lives on the line so that Americans may enjoy economic opportunities, freedom, liberty and justice for all.

The Veterans Business Resource Center is the only center of its kind along the US/Mexico border. The purpose of this center is to help improve the members ' standard of living through start-up, expansion, or acquisition of small businesses, employment, education and training opportunities, establishment or upgrade of VA service connected disability claims. The resource room provides the following, office space, computer and internet access, telephone, fax, copy, scanning and video services.

The Center will also operate as a Veterans Clearinghouse for information and referral services regarding other basic needs including food, shelter and clothing as well as medical and psychological care. It will promote and protect the rights of U.S. Armed Forces Veterans, Active Military Service members, National Guard and Reservists and their families. Additionally, it will provide a safe haven where Veterans Active Duty Military Service Members and their families will be welcomed.

Someday, I want to begin an organization with the help of the people who helped me out. I would call it Butler for Vets, "My Story, Please Listen" has gone worldwide and I would love to continue to making everyone aware of the seriousness of Post Traumatic Stress Disorder. I plan to possibly do some speaking engagements at schools, Vet Centers, VFW and other media outlets.

I feel that as a Soldier from the Iraqi War on Terrorism era, I have a pretty good outlook on how to slow this disease (PTSD) down before it turns into an epidemic. First thing is that I would ask the government to implement a thirty to forty five day evaluation of all military personnel returning to their home duty station. This is to evaluate what type of ailments these Soldiers are returning home with, and then set them up with the local hospital and VA. Give these Soldiers and family members the adequate information needed such as The Vet Center, Veterans of Foreign Affairs, Texas Workforce Center, The Crisis Hotline, The GI Forum and other organizations to assist family and Soldiers. Some of the programs I have noted, I was not informed about, so let's stop playing with the lives of the Soldiers, families and the community. Let's wake up before it is too late. Our Veteran Soldiers should not have to come home to fight another war.

PFC Curtis Butler III – Hanau, Germany 2003-05
Security Dept. under General Dempsey

Why is it we are heroes in wartime, when we return home to the country we love we are treated like the Vietnam Veterans were treated when they returned to the country they love? Is this how our nation treats our Veterans? Well, I just want to say "thank you, America, the land of the free". Free to not help Veterans that ask for assistance, free to be homeless and live under bridges and overpasses after we fought a hard war. I say thank you for assisting us once again so that we all can be free. How many times have you seen a homeless person with a sign saying "I need food" or "I am hungry"? Do we as human beings stop to lend a hand, or do we act like we do not see what is going on around us? Remember, America, Jesus was dressed like some of these homeless people. How do you know that you did not pass Jesus by?

Mr. President, I have a question for you and for Congress, the House and the Senate. How is it that these corporations that messed up get funds on a bail out but the Veterans who helped fight for your freedom cannot receive the funds they need to survive? The last history book I read never mentioned that these corporations were fighting for your freedom, Mr. President and staff members, why is that? When you say the Pledge of Allegiance to the Flag, do you guys really believe what you say? If you did, there would not be any homeless Veterans, so stop saying something that you do not mean or live by.

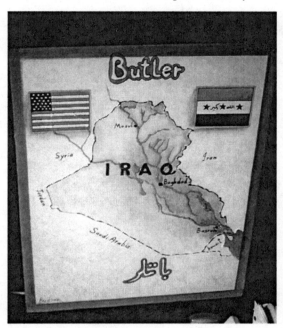

A map of Iraq with name spelled in Arabic - 2003

Mr. President, your staff recently purchased three private jets. Congress just chastised these corporations for flying to Washington to speak about receiving a bail out, while you guys spent tax-payers money on jets. The flight for three planes by the Corporate CEO's was around twenty thousand dollars each one way. Why? Mr. President, was this purchase a want or a need? Sir, I think and the public would agree that it was greed. Your staff should fly first class; it would be cheaper than wasting tax-payers money on a twenty thousand dollar plane ride. You all are too comfortable up in Washington D.C. It is time to close the revolving doors. You said in your speech, it is time for change. These Veterans have been waiting for change for over thirty years. Aren't you guys in D.C. embarrassed over this? And we call America the "Land of The Free". Free to have our Veterans homeless, free to have our Veterans denied benefits because something was not in the records, or because there are no records. "Wake up America, We are Falling Behind".

This question goes to all our Presidents still living. Why is it that when war breaks out, we give that country money to rebuild. Who is giving us money for Pearl Harbor and the World Trade Center and other disasters that occurred?

Why is it that America is always cleaning up someone else's house, while ours is left dirty? America always runs to help others in need. What about the Veterans who fought and are still fighting for freedom? America's military personnel should never be put on the back burner. If there are funds left over after helping the military, then we can assist the other countries, but take care of home first.

Airman First Class Mendoza and Carlos Rivera,
President, Veterans Business Association

I say we take a vote on this, if the Veterans will not be able to receive their disability funds, then pull them out of the War and put the President who are still living and their staff in their place, but please do not come back disabled because you might be in trouble. This is no joke, I am serious, use common sense, change these policies, PLEASE.

One day I would like to meet you, Mr. President, and see if we can brainstorm some ideas so that we can help our Veterans. Do you know that in three to five years the number of our homeless veterans will be more than what we have fighting in the War? The reason for this is that the VA restraints are so tight, that when a Veteran comes in with their forms for disability, they get denied. Is that the VA's favorite word?

Why must Veterans come home from a war to fight another one with the VA? You say we are Heroes in the eyes of the American people, but when it comes to the VA, are they not Americans too? What's up with having people meet us at the airports and have parades for us? Is that a political move or do you really care? Why is it when we have these parades, why must the Soldiers march? They marched already for fifteen months. Let the Soldiers sit in the stands and enjoy their accomplishments and have the people march.

Mr. President, when I walk into the VA I think I am back home going through the Holland Tunnel. Don't get me wrong, I love my hometown of Brooklyn, New York but the VA needs more lights and friendlier colors on the walls and paintings, banners that say "WELCOME HOME VETERANS". VA physicians need to be more understanding, kinder, and they need to listen to the Vets, if you listen, you will hear their stories and be able to diagnose their symptoms. BE PATIENT! I always say you cannot learn anything with a closed book in front of you. Open up to your patients, give eye contact, and do not come to work just for a pay check. Help the Vet who allows you to come to work every day.

"Wake up America, We're falling behind".

Wake up America, we are running around in circles like a dog chasing his tail. What happened to it takes a village to raise a child? How many villages would it take to stop homelessness and hunger for our Veterans and civilians alike? Can we close the Revolving Doors? I have.

CHAPTER FIVE
Critical Thinking in the Military

Today we will explore the critical thinking[1] of a Sergeant in the war zone and a Lieutenant who just graduated from West Point Academy and have never been in a war zone. In my report, the evaluation will show that there truly is not that much difference, but many emotions run wild.

The Lieutenant in the war zone will speak about land navigation and the importance of map reading for the survival of the team, or convoy.

The Lieutenant will enlighten us on lessons learned about the war zone and how other now how to take healthy criticism. It only helps countries look at the United States.

While stationed at Baghdad International Airport (BIAP), critical thinking was a daily task for the U.S. Soldiers. As Non-Commissioned Officers (NCO's) training of Soldiers and officers in many aspects of global warfare we have dealt with all lifestyles, meaning we have different ways of doing the same job at hand. In any job that we did, there was conflict which ends up in critical thinking between team members. At BIAP, I was teamed up with officers, Soldiers and other high ranking NCO's. Our mission was to make sure that our team could function at any level. NCOs would do briefings which sometimes got heated over how you instructed your team members and we had to know how to take healthy criticism. It only helps you to become a better leader. In a war zone, you always have to keep a level head because you and your team are all you have when out on patrol. Each one is counting on the other member to bring him or her back alive. For example if you are instructing Soldiers on map reading and land navigation, you

---

1   "Critical thinking is the intellectually disciplined process of actively and skillfully conceptualizing, applying, analyzing, synthesizing and/or evaluating information gathered from, or generated by, observation, experience, reflection, reasoning, or communication, as a guide to belief and action". (Scriven, 1996)

may forget to instruct them on something that may be critical in a life or death situation. Therefore you have to use critical thinking and go over your location, terrain, toad and weather conditions.

Did you know reading a map has as many as seventy parts; I will only go over the seven colors of a Map. Black indicates cultural (man-made) features, such as buildings and roads. Red-Brown is combined to identify cultural features, all relief features, non-surveyed spot elevation and elevation, such as contour lines on red-light readable maps. Blue identifies hydrograph or water features, such as lakes, swamps, rivers and drainage. Green identifies vegetation with military significance, such as woods, orchards and vineyards. Brown identifies all relief features and elevation, such s contours on older edition maps and cultivated

land on red light readable maps. Red classifies cultural features such as populated areas, main roads and boundaries on older maps[2]. Occasionally, other colors may be used to show special information. These points are indicated in the marginal information. While on patrol, or going from one location to another, make sure all team members know points

2   References: Land Navigation/Map Reading FM 3-25-26 Thursday, March 5, 2009.

and locations on the map. The reason for this is if something bad goes down and your navigation person is hit with enemy fire, someone will have to take his or her place. This goes for everyone on the team and all the different job assignments, driver, gunner and security personnel who are assigned to the high ranking NCO or officer.

Now I will describe the critical thinking of a Lieutenant who has just graduated from West Pont Academy.

Initially, the Lieutenant was convinced that the war in Iraq was retaliation to 911. He thought that we were going after the coordinator of the 911 attacks. However, as time went on, the reasons and justifications started to vary.

What the Lieutenant was thinking is that we made a mistake when invading Iraq. Nonetheless, he believed that going into Iraq was inevitable. Many people continue to argue on whether the invasion was right or wrong. The Lieutenant believed we should focus our efforts on feasible solutions that will help solve the problem we have created over in Iraq.

There is a difference because politics and war are very conflicting. As a result, what we are told is usually different from what is really happening. The biggest lesson the Lieutenant got

Rom the war in Iraq is that as a nation, as the most powerful nation in the world, we must make responsible decisions. Every action must be thought out thoroughly because when we act, the world is affected. Just like the law of physics. "For every action, there is a reaction". I think we forgot all that.

SPC Curtis Butler III meritorious service and dedication award

The next generation of my family, Vanessa, Akil,
Curtis, Jackie, Anthony, Victoria and Michelle.

CHAPTER SIX
Curtis Butler III Like Him or Love Him

If possible, I will try to give similarities and differences of my grand-parents, parents and my era in relations to education, religion, income, occupation and political participation.

Both my Grandparents worked in order to put food on the table for their six children. My Grandmother would come home and cook a meal after returning from a hard days' work. The money back then was minimum and barely enough to take care of a family of six, but they made it work. There was no fancy technology back then; my aunts and Dad were the remote control for the television and the answering machine for the phone. They were my inspiration.

My Grandparents raised six kids back during the depression and World War II. Granddad was a World War II Veteran. After returning home, Granddad worked as a mechanic until retiring in 1986. Grandma worked as a cook and worked side by side with a French Chef who created "The Famous Charleston She-Crab Soup".

Back then, they made very little money and they dealt with racism. My grandparents managed their funds well. They had a wants and needs method, most of the time it was a need. My aunts would pass their clothing down to the next sibling. My Dad told me he would put cardboard in his wholly sneakers in order to keep his feet dry from the rain. My Grandparents always kept food on the table and they sat down together and enjoyed a good hot meal prepared by my Grandma.

When it was time to do homework, my Dad and aunts relied on one another because my Grandparents had very little education. My Grandparents made sure that my Dad and aunts went to church. They were very spiritual people. Church is where we learned who is the Alfa and the Omega, which is GOD. My Dad and aunts learned how to read the bible and understood what was read. My Grandparents did their best to raise six children in a different era where blacks were not accepted as human beings. They taught my Dad and aunts how to love and respect their elders.

I did not really know my Mom; my Grandparents did the best they could in raising me, because my Dad was not around. They made sure I ate, were clothed, went to school and went to church and bible study. I had no choice. They ruled with an iron hand and I'm glad they did.

My Grandmother was the guidance counselor who took care of her student, me, her Grandson. When I would get hurt Grandma would fix it by giving me a snack and holding me, telling me that I would be alright because Grandma loves you.

My Grandfather was a handsome man, was hard working and smart. He could fix anything and had very little education. He was a real man that provided and made sure we had everything we needed to survive.

As I got older, I lived with my Dad, his wife and daughter. It was okay at first. His wife used to buy me clothes and showed me love. My Dad really did not know how to be a father. He would punish me and show his authority. Things were not well and I was sent with my aunts who took care of me.

Painting of daughters Latasha Butler & Sharniece Butler

My aunts were loving people and made sure I had what I needed to stay alive. Clothes, food and rent in New York City were not cheap, but they managed to take care of a family member in need. They never knew how embarrassed I was, but I loved them in return.

Well, I can tell you, I did not cope with my Post Traumatic Stress Disorder very well. I just knew that I was always mad as hell. Half the time I did not know why I was mad, some of the issues I had I had no control over it. It took me awhile to figure out why be mad at what you do not have control over.

Going to the Veterans Administration was like going to the funeral home, the lights, when you walked in were dimly lit, and the walls are one solid color. It is like no life when walking in. If you've been to the VA you know what I am talking about.

I am going to assist the VA with a little knowledge when dealing with Veterans because they have forgotten they work for us. Ii really think some of the workers come for a pay check and a damn if I do and if I don't attitude.

It is like when you got to school, you sit at a desk and you take out your books, but if you do not open them how can you learn. The physician sits at their desk and the Veteran comes in and he is the book. It would benefit to listen to the Soldier's story because they are going to tell you important information. The physicians cold give the Veteran a better description on dealing with the situation if we need to see other specialists for testing. When you do not listen to us we get really offensive and we say and do things that bring a red flag to the situation.

This is what you do not want to do, make promises of harming, or threaten to do harm to the staff. I was listed as a woman hater for one year on the bad boy list.

Now, I have security everywhere I go when entering the VA. All we want when we come into the VA is to be heard and respected. In a way I was wrong for what I did and they were wrong on not giving me certain tests that I asked for because I knew something was wrong with me. My behavior was at a dangerous level. All I wanted to do was kill and it did not matter who it was at the time. If you did something to me that I did not like, I wanted to do bodily harm to you.

If you know people like this get them help immediately. I had a KFOX employee ask me "what about a person my age having PTSD". I told them size and age does not matter, you have unbelievable strength at times and all you want to do is seek and destroy. At a military hospital I was told by my ex-fiancé and medical staff that I damaged some rooms and the reason for this was I had a migraine and I actually was trying to kill myself. I did so many screwed up stuff because I had guilt for the Soldiers that got killed in the War Zone. I called my Aunt Sam and told her I would take that Soldier's place because they were young and wanted to start a family, or they were young and had a family. I told my Aunt Sam that my kids are almost grown and I have lived my life. My aunt responded if those Soldiers had it their way, they would wish they were alive.

My ex-fiancé told me while she was sitting down, that I lifted her up in the air, while she was holding on to my leg and arm I became uncontrollable. She had bruises on her and I asked her what happened to you? My ex answered "you did this". To this day, I still do not recall that incident. I was then taken to the psychiatric ward and admitted for approximately two weeks, at my ex request. I think my ex was really scared of me, which cuts deep in my soul when a person loves you and you do not want to love back. I do not even know if I apologized to her. So I will say it now, I apologize to you and to my step daughter.

My ex-fiancé even told me that she was putting her arm around me when I was sleeping and that I grabbed her arm while still asleep and she got scared. She said my response was "I'm sorry" and then I went back to sleep. Let your family members know what's going on. If my ex had not said anything to me, I do not know what the outcome would have been, but thank God that I released her in my sleep.

I know we all miss our spouse, but make sure they are ready for the family life after you spent fifteen months in the War Zone. It will be difficult to explain how you get in-jured while sleeping with your loved one. Flashbacks occur with me all the time, crying for no apparent reason, mood swings and not caring about a sole. These things are normal for us because of situations that have oc-curred in the past fifteen months. I know that I am not the only one go-ing through this. I see the same looks on Soldiers' faces when I go to my appointments at the VA. It is a cold blank stare that can cut into your skin deep down to the bone, and you get this tunnel vision where everything around you gets dark and you hear no sounds. That is the closest I want to get to death without dying. You cannot reach out to anyone in this stage, it is like you are trying to say something but you cannot hear the words but you know you're saying something. This is what we live with everyday. I still see rats run around the room and when I ask people "did you see that rat?" they look at me and say stop tripping. But this is very real to us, it's like our mind is playing tricks or a bad joke. It's like we have dancing devils in our head.

Post Traumatic Stress Disorder is not a military issue; it is a world problem. Our government need not put this on the back burner; like they did with the Veterans past and present on providing them with

28

their disability checks. We have to realize that it takes a special kind of person to deal with a person or a Soldier suffering from PTSD. Sometimes, we lose the friend or family member and sometimes, we don't because of Gods' grace. I had my family and different organizations assist me in controlling my disease. God sends people in your life for different reasons, but you have to listen for his voice, so you know which person is there to help you in different situations.

Curtis with Cousin Anthony Spencer

My younger brother is a great man to his wife and beautiful daughter. He and his wife straightened me out a couple of times when I was thinking about doing some off the wall stuff.

My sister is a fantastic wife and mother to her husband and handsome son. My cousin and his beautiful wife would talk to me when I was down. My Mother and a host of family members helped me when I was really in left field. We would speak on the phone until they knew I was deflating my thoughts of doing anything foolish.

I would speak of getting into a gun battle with cops, which is called suicide by police. My mind, body, soul and spirit were going bunkers. I was just an empty shell waiting to wither away into nothing and was ready to roll over and die.

This is how the VA makes me feel, like I am nothing, like I am bothering them at their job. Our government needs to put more of our tax payers' money into the VA and stop sending it to other countries. Do any of you tax payers receive any extra checks during tax return? I tell you why you don't because our government pockets most of it. It's all about what the other countries can do and how much returns are coming back to our government in "God We Trust".

Painting of Curtis' brother Akil Childs and sister-in-law Rikki Childs

America, how can we be broke, by lending funds that we do not have to our neighboring country? This is how I deal with my Post Traumatic Stress Disorder; I find the fallacies in our government, then I put it down on paper and ask when our government will stop lying to us.

America, this Nobel Peace Prize should have gone to a Soldier who laid down their life for our Freedom and the sacrifice they did for the family and friends. America, we need to wake up, we need to look at ourselves and learn the laws of the land so that we stop being used like pawn in a chess game.

When you have to fight for your benefits that you earned fighting a War, I call that a checkmate. When you do not have proper medical, I call that checkmate. When you cannot pay your bills, I call that checkmate. We, as a nation have been disrespecting our military Soldiers and putting the Heroes on the back burner for over thirty plus years and now we are doing this to our Soldiers of today. The heck, it's time for a change, let's close the revolving doors and start doing something right now.

First thing I had to do was pray and ask for forgiveness from my Heavenly Father. My heart was full of hate. I lost many Soldier friends that are no longer here and hurt from things I did and what life had thrown at me. Post Traumatic Stress Disorder takes over your body if you let it, you have to fight and control your body, mind, spirit and soul.

You have to always put yourself in a different place. Find a place in your home where you have things that put a smile on your face, like a room with pictures of a family member or members and friends, then close your eyes and think pleasant thoughts while you meditate. Have you an outer body experience. Take deep breaths and think pleasant and positive thoughts. Remember Rome was not built in a day, this takes time and patience.

Soldiers and family members will tell someone that something is wrong no matter what the response is. Document your conversation; this is your paper trail if people tell you that you are not the same. These are signs that I heard and ignored from family and friends and I was a time bomb that was ready to explode at any given time.

We are so comfortable with ourselves that sometime we brush tings off and tell people that we are alright when we are not. I guess that is the human side of us all, I know I am guilty of this. It is like we want to act tough when things are not quite right when we have obligations and responsibilities that hand over our heads every day.

Let us not forget about the civilian family members of Soldiers, they are not immune from PTSD and they need treatment as well. This can also help the Soldiers when they return from the War zone. I will explain; when Soldiers are getting ready to deploy, our government or representatives should contact the Veterans Administration, military and surrounding hospitals, churches, local, state, county and federal agencies and other organizations to assist with this disease we call PTSD.

PFC Curtis Butler III, Baghdad. 2003-2005
Security Department under General Dempsey

The family members should be allowed to speak with a mental health care provider when a member of the family getting ready to deploy to the War Zone for approximately fifteen months. If the Soldiers go to the mental health with family members, they can put their feeling out on the table without being looked at differently by others. We all play that tough role, but we need to be real with ourselves. We are humans; things happen sometimes, we just have to let it play out.

When a Soldier knows that their loved ones are being taken care of, bills being paid, the family members are still going to mental health so that they can be strong for their Soldier in harm's way. Believe it or not, this takes off a lot of stress for the Soldier and family.

We need to have seminars to that our physicians can provide adequate care to our Veterans and family members. Our government needs to stop putting Veterans last. If it was not four us Veterans, you may not be in these positions that you are in now. Our Veterans have a hard time, provide adequate funding. I keep hearing that we are in a deficit, so why are we sending tax payers money to other countries? Our tax money needs to work for us. Politicians stop padding your pockets with the theory, "I wash your back you wash my back" for companies and other countries needing assistance. Work for the American people who voted you into office who need your assistance more than the big companies and countries you are supporting now.

I would not change my life because God gave me this hand and I had to know how to play it. If it was not for all of those trials and tribulations, I might not have written "My Story Please Listen" which is receiving worldwide attention. All of these papers make up Curtis Butler III. Thank you and God Bless!!

CHAPTER SEVEN
My Story Please Listen

My barrier would be Post Traumatic Stress Disorder (PTSD), I will explain the different changes in my life after returning home from the War Zone and how it derails me in everyday life. Having the support of doctors, family and friends, they are now helping me cope with many issues and demons that lurk in my mind, body, soul and spirit. This was not so when I returned home. People say prayer helps, which I am not knocking, it is like the military saying, "Hurry up and wait", meaning be patient. I will give you insight on the security measures used on me when I enter any Veterans Building Administration.

When I returned home from the war, they assigned me to Team B. This is where another explosion happened. My nurse stated that my medical records did not indicate that I had PTSD. I, then, proceeded to tell the workers at the VA that I would wait in the parking lot and choke the shit out of that nurse. Reason was that I came to my physician for help, instead she like slapped me in the face which angered me. I then asked to speak with the VA Advocate Liaison. I spoke to the advocate liaison about the incompetence of the Nurse and her lack of knowledge of PTSD. The advocate liaison told me that she would assign me to another doctor from Team B. This doctor listened to what I had to say and takes measures to help me cope with my situation. Other organizations that are assisting me are the Vet Center, the Veterans Service Representative in Waco, Texas and the Veterans Service Representative in El Paso, Texas.

When I filed the paper work and the statement I made about the nurse, I was put on the alert list. This means every time I enter the VA security has to accompany me to all my appointments for one year.

I do not claim to be a doctor, but

I based my thinking that I am a totally different person from what friends and family have told me and what they have seen. I am like a time bomb just waiting to explode and do not even know why. This is what I told the Advocate Liaison and my two specialists. Flash backs haunt me due to activities that happened in Baghdad with my unit 4/1 Calvary and 1st Armored Division. Between the units, I knew over 100 Soldiers got killed, mostly by Improvised Explosive Devices (IED). Most of the bodies came back mangled or a couple of pieces missing. Some Soldiers I would see and speak to them. I see these Soldiers when I go to sleep and I have night terrors. I am taken back to the war zone and find myself fighting the enemies to the death. This is one of many dreams that sticks in my head, in my dream where detaining the Iraqi enemies, securing them with tie bands. As I approached the enemy, he turns around and shoots me point blank range in my chest. Last thing I remembered was a Soldier yelling "man down" and I hear shots ring out. I do not know if the Soldiers killed the enemy, then I wake up with a pounding heart, breathing hard and sweating. My ex-fiancé used to tell me that I would talk in my sleep about injured Soldiers in my unit.

She also told me that I grabbed her arm hard while I was asleep and all she was doing was trying to cuddle. At that time, I was having night terrors that I am still fighting today. I end up hurting my ex fiancé. I lost her and my stepdaughter by popping pills prescribed by the VA, drinking and cheating. I attempted suicide when I took too many pills in order to get rid of a bad migraine. I did not love anyone or myself. I thought the world would be better without me. My ex fiancé had me committed to William Beaumont Psychiatrist Ward for about two weeks. The doctor told me that I went on a rampage and tore up two rooms in less than five minutes. I must have blacked out because I do not remember anything.

An incident happened one time I was in the doctor's office being examined. As the doctor talked to me, she came around behind me. That startled me. At the time, unknowingly, I told the doctor I would have killed you thinking you were the enemy. I regained my composure right away.

At that time, in my mind, I also wanted to kill my Dad for things done wrong to my brother and sister. I wanted to do harm to everyone that harmed me. Some military personnel had me relieved of duties when I was in my prime, moving up the NCO chain. I was hoping to make it to the Sergeant Major Academy. I am a decorated Soldier and an outstanding NCO. All it took was some bad words by some officers and I'm a goner.

I have a new girlfriend, and I now, speak with my Dad and we tell one another "I love you". I am working hard to make the relationship work but it's hard for me, it is as if I have to learn how to love again and most of all to love myself. I have great friends from my class and other retired Soldiers that are assisting me with my many problems fighting the VA claims office in Waco, Texas.

In May of 2007, I was stationed in Texas. When arriving to my unit, I knew things were not right, Soldiers walking around like they had no place where to go.

I saw a private talking back to a Sergeant and they let them get away with it. A female private wanted to come over to my house and I refused. We had a few mean words in front of other Soldiers.

Another Soldier that did not like me because when I did room inspection, I embarrassed her about her living area. I wanted them to know that I was not a push over Sergeant and that I wanted the section looking good at all times. The other Sergeant would be more lenient and tell me if these Soldiers were not under my command, do not check on them. I did not understand the warning because as a Non Commissioned Officer you are supposed to take care of all the Soldiers. They told me that they have problems and issues; well our job was to make sure we helped the Soldiers with problems and issues. Then I met a lady Sergeant, she was a class act at the time. I did not know anything about her. She was friendly and wanted to help me out in my new unit. I would go with her to pick her kids from the day care center. We would hang out in the office or go to different offices to pick up things or just to introduce me to the staff. A couple of months later, I was in the office with her and I gave her a kiss behind the neck. She did not say a thing about it.

Two privates that I made friends with were tolerant of our joking and laughing together. I thought we were good friends. A month after we met, I was helping them load up some equipment. One of the privates seemed upset. I walked up to her and asked "are you all right?" She was having trouble tying of her boots and I helped her. Playfully, I patted her on the leg. She walks away and slams the door shut.

I get called into the office, the Lieutenant wanted to see me about this harassment charges filed by the two privates. I entered the office and was asked to explain my side of the story. I said how can I be up on charges when you have the Private getting her ass whooped by the Captain's wife for sleeping with her husband and you have other Soldiers wives wanting to whoop on her for trying to sleep with other Soldiers husbands. For the Private to explain when she was sitting in the Light Mobile Terain Vehicle I patted the top of her leg. She claimed that I tried to touch her privates. At that time that issue was dropped and they said it was over because they knew when I demonstrated the actions it was not possible for me to do what she said when both legs are in the vehicle and I'm standing flat on the ground. I let them know my height is 5'9".

Here is where the problems lay. Our first Commander and First Sergeant was a joke and the Lieutenant Colonel and Sergeant Major knew this and did nothing about it. They could have put a lot of this to rest, but instead they asked me if I had witnesses to testify in my behalf. I did not know anyone; I just got to this base. Time has passed

now; the rumors are floating about me beating this harassment charge. We get to California for training before we head to the War Zone. I get investigated on charges that they open up again that I just beat. I answered the questions truthfully and I get burned for adultery and maltreatment of Soldiers. I still did my training at that time preparing meals for Soldiers in my unit.

In Kuwait City I may have said some things to Private A that should not have been said. I was wrong and it was unprofessional of me as an NCO. I am human, I make mistakes and I will make mistakes until we leave this earth.

Now, in Iraq, Private A disobeyed a direct order and I told her that she had to write a five hundred word essay on "Why You Should Not Disrespect a Non Commissioned Officer". Here is the catch; Private A told Soldiers and the chain of command that I told her that I would give her fifteen hundred dollars and she would not have to write the essay.

But she still wrote the essay and the chain of command did not check with finance about the funds which I will speak about later. Some Soldiers that were bunking with me said that I had adult movies on my computer, which I did. Half of the Soldiers, including officers had adult movies. I received a Summary Court Marshall and a General Discharge under Honorable Conditions. At the trial I was escorted by two Sergeants. As the trial started the witness and Private A forgot what they wrote. If these things happened they would have remembered dates and time. The investigator would have known I took fifteen hundred dollars on that date and time. None of that happened.

Did you know that you cannot get out fifteen hundred dollars from finances in the War Zone? Did you know the max amount at that time was around five hundred dollars amount? The reason why no one knew was because nobody checked. The case would have been dropped for falsifying a statement and that Soldier would have been in confinement. How many of you Soldiers would have been in confinement or received an Article 15 or Article 134. I guess that was a blow to you Soldiers' egos.

I could not get one witness to testify because they said they did not want to get involved. I have a couple of years left to serve and I have a family to feed. I could not get mad if they didn't want to testify. To those Soldiers I say "It's okay". My attorney advised me to take a plea deal so that I could go on with my life. Or I would face a trial knowing that I did not have witnesses to testify on my behalf. He told me that I would have a record and loose all my benefits as a Veteran which was a kick in the teeth. Sometimes, in life you have to do things that you would not normally do so that justice can prevail. My two Sergeant escorts knew about the situation but said nothing either. I did in a way have witnesses but they left a falling comrade behind, which is a military term.

After everything was said and done, I convoyed up to Talafar, Iraq. When I got there some of the Sergeants were saying "we were trying, to get you up her, but they got you man". They said that's why we are glad we're here because the chain of command is crooked as hell and that they knew what was going on and all they did was work to make the next rank.

I did what was told in Talafar. I had no problems with anybody there. I had guard duty at the front gate almost every night and did not complain after everything was said and done. I am still treated like and NCO even though I was not an NCO anymore. They had told me once an NCO always an NCO. I had been with this unit a short time and Soldiers there really did not get a chance to know me. I looked on the blog and it said I was a joke, not a real NCO. I couldn't train Soldiers because I was a sexual predator and that I should not be the voice of Veterans. I took those comments and I kept it moving. People like them want me to continue to live in the past but I refused. They may be the one that has a War baby and she is someone else's wife. You may be the wife of a Soldier that had a War baby from another Soldier. You can't go on television and say that.

Then they brought my computer and camera back, some of my pictures that I had of Soldiers with other Soldiers' spouses were erased. I wonder why, this is the bias that went on in my military investigation. I guess they did not tell the Soldiers about that and how my trial was botched. I consider it a rush job. When I told my chain of command that the Soldiers I was living with had adult movies, they said they did not find any. If they checked the computer down to the memory, they would have seen it, but they didn't.

Higher ups knew that some Soldiers were sleeping with other Soldiers and that they were married. Now can you get pregnant in the War Zone and your spouse is in the states? Your chain of command walks in on you and two female Soldiers, one married, and are in bed and nothing happens. If this is not biased and scandalous, then what is?

40

One can say I got my battle buddy's wife or my friend's wife pregnant. They are in your face one day and banging a wife the next day. You Soldiers kill me you talk the talk, walk the walk, and then tell your buddies that the kid is not theirs. I'm on the news trying to do right, trying to make a change and you still want to throw rocks at me. You kicked my ass in Iraq, I licked my wounds and now I'm taking back my life. All it takes for the female Soldiers to wake up and smell the coffee and we will see what you would do in your situation.

Female Soldiers sleeping with your boy toys or your husband's homeboy, then going home for vacation saying that the husband got you pregnant. I say what give you the right to throw rocks at me. My whole trial was a joke. Now let' see you go to trial, what are you going to say. I did not know he was married, or the condom broke. Do not get me wrong, I'm not upset at any of the Soldiers. I said I did say some things that I shouldn't have but now it's time for me to set the record straight. Some of you trick Soldiers come out of the closet and take a deep breath. Are you worried what people are going to think and say? It was all good when it was all on me, like it was said on the blog. I'm calling out the higher chain of command also. I would love for Congress to call all of you trick officers and non commissioned officers out and put you guys on display in front of your peers.

The things that I'm writing about is not for all Soldiers, we have good ones. These Soldiers know who I am talking about. If you want to be honest about everything, let people know that you lied. You got away with it back then. This book might open all wounds again, and then you will be getting the funny looks I had been getting since 2007. You will have people stop speaking to you like they did to me.

Do you know that while in the War Zone when the enemies are on the outside of the Forward Operation Base and you have Soldiers that disown you, that that is a very bad feeling when you feel like a rat up against the wall? I walked around at night, did not have a sole to speak to me in Mosul. Do you know how scary that shit was; just call my aunts and uncles.

I was suicidal because no one would testify on my behalf. It was like being in enemy territory by myself and everyone around me got killed. I was stuck in a spot until it was time for me to depart.

Put yourself in that position for one hour. Stand in a dark uncomfortable place. I guarantee you would not be a happy camper. No Soldier should ever feel that way. I do not want pay back, I want Congress to help clear my name and if they see fit, to return my rank and back pay. That would be appreciated.

Some Soldiers knew I could not win that fight down range. My uncle said for me to fight when I get back on solid ground. Now, I am fighting to restore my families' name. I am not asking for Congress to reinstate back into the military, I want Congress to oversee the investigations with the military and not let the Brigades do any more investigation because biases may and have occurred. I would also like for Congress to look into those four Soldiers from the same base in Texas who have similar charges. The so called investigation that was done in California does not in any way shape or form works in favor of the accused. Without any witnesses you're gone and your military career is history. How many Soldiers do you know or herd of that when they read over the trail notes found a lot of discrepancies. It really makes you think. I hope this does not happen to you. I hope someone steps up to the plate instead of taking the back seat.

Now, I have a team backing me now and reviewing my case. I hope to also get my General under Honorable changed back to an Honorable Discharge with the help of the President of the United States.

What Soldiers do not know about me:
Military Experience: 1989-1991
Two Honorable Discharges, 2002-2007
Once General under Honorable Discharge

Security Experience: During my tour in 2003 Baghdad, I supervised more than two hundred and fifty Iraqi Nationals. I was part of General Dempsey Security Staff and assisted in providing security for President Bush and Secretary of State Condoleezza Rice. I was given the nickname Lock and Load.

Weapons Experience: The M-4, M-16, M-249 SAW, 50 Cal, and the 9MM. I have over a thousand hours training, breaking down and putting these weapons back together and qualifying as a sharpshooter.

Instructing Experience Baghdad 2003: Instructing Soldiers on security procedures while on the FOB, when Iraqi Laborers built LSA IRON.

Supervisor Experience: While attached to the 1st A.D. Commandant

Section, I served as the supervisor for the Iraqi nationals, providing daily custodial operations in and around the Baghdad International Airport.

Procedural Writing Experience: I helped revised the Standard Operation Procedures for the security of Baghdad International Airport for the incoming Soldiers, dignitaries and Iraqi Nationals.

My drive and positive attitude increased the proficiency of the organization in a short period of time. My dedication to duty and mission accomplished provided motivation and inspiration for my peers and superiors alike. My attention to detail, enthusiasm and indomitable spirit was instilled within my peers. My actions as a combat Soldier marked me as a true leader and hero who served his nation with pride and distinction.

Decorations, Medals, Badges, Citations and Campaign Ribbons Awarded or Authorized:
    Army Commendation Medal (2nd AWARD OLC)
    Army Achievement Medal
    Valorous Unit Award
    Army Good Conduct Medal
    National Defense Service Medal with Bronze Star
    Global War on Terrorism Expeditionary Medal
    Global War on Terrorism Service Medal
    Iraq Campaign Medal
    Army Service Ribbon
    Kuwait and Iraq Overseas Service Ribbon (2nd AWARD)

Military Education:
    Field Sanitation Team Course
    Individual Readiness Training Course
    Master Drivers Training Course

Ribbons: I have five ribbons for Culinary Arts Competition won in Hanau, Germany.

A plaque that says June 2003-April 2006
HHC/2-501st Avn Regt. 1st A.D.

FOR MERITORIOUS SERVICE, DEDICATION AND SUP-
PORT OF THE 4ᵀᴴ BDE, JFK CONSOLIDATED DINING FA-
CILITY HANAU, GERMANY

Received over fifty coins for providing security for varies dignitaries
and for helping to win numerous awards in the food service area.

Promoted to Sergeant 2006.

Achievements: PFC Butler superbly executed duties as a SAW gunner
for the Division's G Section on five separate occasions during combat
patrols in Baghdad, Iraq. PFC Butler was diligent, competent crew
member and was requested by name due to his keen situational aware-
ness and enthusiastic attitude. During his tenure he performed his duties admirable receiving coins and recognition from various VIP's.

25 April 2004: PFC Butler's performance was instrumental in the
unit's safe redeployment from and back to Baghdad, Iraq. His extraordinary efforts were vital during the Battalion's 1300 kilometer round
trip convoy from Baghdad, Iraq to Kuwait and back through hostile
areas without incident or injuries. His attention to detail, enthusiasm
and indomitable spirit was instilled within his peers. PFC Butler's actions as a combat Soldier marked him as a true leader and hero who
served his nation with pride and distinction.

25 April 2004: SPC Butler's untiring dedication to duty and outstanding performance were key factors in the overall success of the Culinary
Arts Competition. With his attention to detail, initiative and "Can do"
attitude, SPC Butler played a key role in the Dining Facility Display
planning.

25 Nov 2004: SPC Butler worked as first cook in a consolidated dining facility during CMTC 05-05. Supporting over 650 Soldiers with
daily per meal. He trained two Soldiers on field food service operations, preparations and safety.

14 March 2005: While maintaining accountability of all Class I subsistence, SPC Butler worked long and continuous hours in rations ensuring that all Class I subsistence were delivered in a timely manner. He

also oversaw the loading and unloading of rations and all breakdowns, ensuring that all perishables were not spoiled or damaged.

14 March 2005: SPC Butler provided outstanding Food Service support for the 4th BDE Dining Facility as a First cook. His motivation and leadership made it possible for his Soldiers to serve over 600 Soldiers daily. SPC Butler's culinary expertise was instrumental in the success of the 4th BDE Thanksgiving Day 2005 outstanding achievement. For his superb display he received a Silver medal for two displays.

18 July 2003 to 2 April 2006: SPC Butler's strong leadership attributes and drive to succeed consistently produced outstanding results. He successfully completed three CMTC rotations and four Battalion Gunneries.

SPC Butler's high standards of food service preparation and Class I operations were commended by his superiors on numerous occasions. The outstanding meals he prepared greatly improved the morale of all the Soldiers who ate them.

18 July 2003 to 2 April 2006: SPC Butler played a key role during the Connelly competition for FY 2005. His ability to focus the energy of his peers was pivotal to the 4thBDE Dining Facility winning the 104th ASG Phillip A. Connelly award for the best Dining Facility. His extraordinary leadership and knowledge brought compliments and high marks from all judges.

18 July 2003 to 2 April 2006: SPC Butler's efforts and drive to excel were evident throughout his tour. His high level of morale was worthy of emulation and he contributed significantly to accomplishment of the unit's mission. His devotion to duty and superior knowledge of many facets of the food service operations, not only resulted in the development f high standards for food service, but also inspired all those with whom he worked.

18 July 2003 to 2 Aril 2006:
    Civilian Education
    Food Protection Management
    Card Expire 2012

University of Phoenix
BSB/A GPA 3.56

While in school, I wrote "Close the Revolving Doors", "Homeless Veterans", "Wake up America We're Falling Behind", "Curtis Butler III Like Him or Love Him" and "Post Traumatic Stress Disorder, all chapters under my book "My Story Please Listen".

Ii put all of my writings into my book "My Story Please Listen". It tells of the wrong things I have done in the military and the different bias and corruption I uncovered in the Army. I speak on political views, religion and family issues that we all have. Two of my writings made the news and also went out on the World Wide Web. "Close the Revolving Doors" and Post Traumatic Stress Disorder "My Story Please Listen" has been interviewed by the local news. I am scheduled for a couple more engagements to discuss my book. Ms. Pam Baker is writing "Eddie's Story". It is a story about her uncle.

On Veterans Day, we prepared a luncheon for the Vietnam Veterans. The staff assisted me in preparing the meal consisting of Mango and Pineapple Glazed Ribs, Baked Beans, Veggies and a medley of fruits. I am honored to have prepared a meal for these heroes who have paved the way so that we can have and enjoy our freedom we so gracefully love.

Mr. President, bring home those heroes and you guys go down and fight the war yourselves. I say to the people of this great country, "We need to veto all of the living Presidents and staff pay until the Veterans get their back pay from thirty plus years ago, including the Iraqi Freedom Veterans".

The last two Presidents have been putting military last when our Soldiers come home beaten and battered. Mr. President, like I called out the VA, I am now calling you out on your words (It's time for a change). Don't you like your freedom? If you do, why are you still cleaning up other counties problems when we have our own problems right here with the "Homeless Veterans", medical, housing, jobs and many other problems? Recently, the VA gave them a twenty-four million dollar bonus. YOU ARE ALL GREEDY.

"Just remember GOD said first on earth, last to pass through the gates of heaven".

El Paso, I have plans for a Homeless Veterans situation. I have a team that wants to put these Veterans in homes and take them to appointments, to job training and prepare them to go back into the work force. I do not know about you El Paso, but I'm tired of seeing our homeless Veterans out there. Help us clean our own backyard. Let's make El Paso a homeless free city. We stand together as one united everybody else will follow. "Close the Revolving Doors, Wake up America, We're Falling Behind".

"Thank you America and GOD BLESS all of our Veterans fighting for freedom".

A heartfelt "thank you" for all of you who believed in me.

I would like to thank God for showing me how to pass my test in life and for giving me the strength to continue. My Father, Curtis Butler Jr., my brother and sister-in-law, Akil, Rikki, thank you for your support. Kenlyne Childs, you are an ANGEL. My Sister and brother in law, Halima and Paul, thank you for the love that you showed me. P J Conerly, I visualize you playing for the Giants like my classmate Dwane Kinnon did in our school class of 1986. Uncle Tony, Aunt (Sam) Jennette that gave me guidance. My cousins, Victoria and Vanessa, Uncle Clarence, Aunt Ann, thank you for helping me. Aunt Gloria, thank you letting cook that fabulous Easter dinner. (Did anyone take pictures? Send me some copies). Aunt Rose, Aunt Mary, thank you for giving me a place to stay when I needed it. To my gown daughters Danielle, Sharniece, Latasha and my grandson Jeramiah, my cousin Anthony, you are my brothers and dear friends. Sonia Spencer, thank you for those serious talks we had. Jackie Frasier, my cousin Michelle, Torry, Taylor, Tyrene and Trinity thank you with all my heart.

Lord, thank you for my extended family that showed me love on the base at Ft. Bliss, Texas, they did not give up on me.

To my extended family of friends, "thank you".

To Bill Sparks, Carlos Rivera, President of the Veterans Business Association, Congressman Reyes and his staff, for all their assistance. The University of Phoenix staff and instructors for letting me express my thoughts in a positive way. Thanks to First Light Credit Union and Wells Fargo, part of my business team. My right hand people, Patricia Sias, my business partner and Hartmut Mueller, good friend and computer genius. Chris Castillo, my business development advisor, Chelle's Event Management and Design, Pam Baker from Custom Sports Cards, Rudy and staff at El Zarape Restaurant, East El Paso Rotary Club, EP Sound Stash, Greater El Paso Chamber of Commerce, Rafael Hernando, Inside Out Youth Club, Spotlight Media

Productions, Veterans Business Association, Veterans Business Resort Center, VICTORY Veterans in Clint, Texas. Willie Jenkins, Freedom Material and Janitorial Services, Jerry Kurryka, Glacier Technologies, John Butler at Goodwill, Lewis Woodyard, Charles, Mike, Gabriel Pedroza and family in August, GA., Ellis White in KCMO, DAV Chapter 187, Adobe Hacienda Dance Hall, Annette Browne and family in Maryland, Vicky Lee from KHEY Radio and Rod, and KFOX. Juan Reyes, Jacarna Shuler, my childhood friend in N.C.

Much love to Able Street and 1st A.D 2nd /501st and the CAV. Without you guys there would not have been "My Story Please Listen". I bet after this someone is listening now.

Curtis visits with brother Akil during break

CHAPTER EIGHT
How I cope with Post Traumatic Stress Disorder

Few people understand the stress we are going through. The anxiety, the nightmares, the feeling of despair and a depressed state of mind as we cope with PTSD.

In the service to our country I and many others went through a period of turmoil suffering the consequences of war. The sleepless nights, the sounds of thunder and the cries of my fellow Soldiers were as traumatic as we could absorb. But returning to our country and being taken care of at the Veterans Clinic was as traumatic as the war itself. Why, because the Doctors at the clinic do not understand us. I know Ii ma not the only one going though this. I see the same looks on the Soldiers faces when I go to the VA Clinic. It is a blank stare that only we can understand.

Post Traumatic Stress Disorder is not just a military issue, it is a world problem that our government has put on the back burner like they did with the Veterans of past wars. We have to realize that it takes a special kind of person to deal with us suffering from PTSD. We need the help of many people including our family members, our church and friends.

God sends people into your life for different reasons but you have to listen to his voice to understand that there is help out there. First thing I had to do was pray and ask forgiveness from my Heavenly Father.

My heart was full of hate. I lost many of my friends in that war and I did things that hurt people but that are what life threw at me. Post Traumatic Stress Disorder takes over your body if you let it. You have to fight to control it with your mind, spirit and soul.

Put yourself in a different place in your mind. Find a place in your surroundings, in your home where you have things that can put your mind at ease, like a room with family pictures. Close your eyes and think of pleasant thoughts while you meditate. Have an outer body experience. Take deep breathes and think pleasant and positive thoughts. It will take time, but it works.

Your friends, family members can tell if something is wrong. They can sense that you are not the same person they once knew. Listen to them, these are signs that I heard and ignored and all this time I was a time bomb ready to explode. We feel so comfortable with ourselves that we brush things off and tell everyone that we are fine when we are not. I know I am guilty of that. It is like we want to act tough when we are not well.

I am beginning to put my life back in order. Here is how I deal with Post Traumatic Stress Disorder.

Post Traumatic Stress Disorder can have a life changing effect on loved one's lives therefore we need to cope with PTSD in the healthiest and most positive way. The stress of PTSD can cause a rippling affect that closes the doors on relationships, the mood of the individual and the people around him. It has the ability to affect your work and school.

PTSD symptoms are different with everyone and are difficult to deal with; it may lead to unhealthy and unsafe ways with coping with the decease including the heavy use of alcohol or drugs. However, there are a number of healthy things we can do to manage PTSD and improve our lives. Being mindful of PTSD is a very good way to cope. Mental health professionals ask that we do these techniques in order to maintain our mental capacities. These exercises may be helpful in getting your mind to keep in touch with the present. It only takes a few minutes of our time.

STEP ONE
Find a quiet and comfortable place. Lie down on you back or sit still with your back straight against your seat. This will release the tension in your shoulders. Relax, let your shoulders drop.

STEP TWO
Close your eyes

STEP THREE
Focus and control your breathing. Pay attention to your body. Breathe in and out slowly. Listen to your body.

STEP FOUR
Continue to focus on your breathing. Imagine you are on your dream vacation with family and friends.

STEP FIVE
If your mind wonders (this is totally normal) see if you can find what took your mind away and slowly work yourself back to the present.

STEP SIX
Continue this exercise for as long as you like. It will defuse you.

Using Self Soothing Skills to Cope with Stress
I am going to give you a tip when you feel yourself getting upset. You need to have an escape from yourself. Seek out social support; this will help you in order to improve your mood.

As we all know, PTSD triggers unpleasant events. Remember we are all accountable for our actions. These are some of the soothing skills I learned to do in order to maintain my control over PTSD.

TOUCH
1. Soak in a nice hot bath.
2. Get a deep tissue massage or use a massage chair.
3. Do stretching exercises.
4. Go for a long swim or walk. Enjoy the surroundings.
5. Put on clothing that feels good to you.
6. Play with a Pet. Animals take the stress off of you.

TASTE
1. Eat a well balanced meal.
2. Eat healthy foods.
3. Sip some hot herbal tea.
4. Such on hard candy.
5. Drink plenty of water.

SMELL
1. Light scented candles, they have a nice smell.
2. Shop for flowers or roses.
3. Take a deep breath of fresh air.

SIGHT

1. Look at pictures of family members or friends.
2. Watch the different shapes of the clouds.
3. Look at old vacation pictures or photos of places you would like to visit.
4. Watch a funny movie or read a good book.

SOUND

1. Listen to some good music, it is relaxing.
2. Say something encouraging to yourself.
3. Sing a song to yourself.

As you do these techniques, focus on the task at hand, we do not want you to hurt yourself or others. We are all family and fighting the same enemy. Believe me when I say this, you are loved. We all need a shoulder to cry on. It does not make us less of a man. We need someone who cares, that can say I love you. We want someone to say, we understand and mean it. PLEASE DO NOT SAY IT IF YOU DO NOT MEAN IT.

Try coming up with as many techniques as possible, it will help you maintain issues that you are coping with. Do these techniques every day. Be true to yourself and your surroundings. I would rather have family and friends visit you at home than at the morgue.

Writing to Cope with Post Traumatic Stress Disorder

I have found this technique to work wonders for me. In my book I thank the University of Phoenix for letting me express myself in writing my thoughts in a professional way. Just start writing. Do not worry about spelling errors. Put all your thoughts and feelings on paper even if it doesn't make sense. This is a very good way to release pressure and tension. You are now showing that PTSD does not control or run your life.

STEPS TO CONTROL PTSD

1. Find a nice quite place. Give yourself some time.
2. Take time to think of what is holding you back.
3. Write about the first feeling and thoughts that come.
4. Once you finished expressing your thoughts, read what you wrote. Look at yourself in the mirror and you will see a change. You will

start to pay more attention to how you feel and act as a result of your writings.

5. Writing about past situations will put a tear in your eyes. Before you know it, you will be making corrections. It happened to me.

6. Save and keep all your journals or writings in a safe place. Your writings may help others suffering from PTSD

Flashbacks that flash back

One thing I tell my doctors is what makes me go off into left field that bring red flags, but as

I mentioned earlier, be real and honest with you. It's okay to cry or scream or yell. I have done these things many times before. Work out in a gym. Hit a punching bag not someone else.

Express yourself. The Veterans Administration tells me I cannot do or say certain things, but if I cannot express myself and my thoughts to the doctor, why go there? If the doctors don't listen of our experience in the war zone how are they going to diagnose our problem?

I am learning how to associate with people again. I still have issues in going to the store or malls.

I try to go grocery shopping around midnight or early morning. I tried going to the movies but broke out in a cold sweat. To this day, I have not gone to the movies.

Make sure you can identify early warning signs of reactions; they can be unpredictable and uncontrollable. I just started crying and my heart beat became faster. You need someone you trust to help you get back to the present. I have found someone to help me and I am very thankful for that.

These are some grounding techniques that will help when you find yourself slipping into the dark side.

TOUCH

Grip something really cold from the freezer. It will focus your thoughts to the present, which is the cold object in your hand.

TASTE

Bite into something bitter. It will produce a strong sensation in your mouth and bring you back to reality.

SMELL

Take a real hot pepper, smell and it will catch you from slipping into a flashback.

SIGHT

✓ Take inventory of your surroundings.
✓ Listen to the noises around you.
✓ Write down what triggers your PTSD. These charts or documents can help the doctor assist you.
✓ We must be aware of the many internal triggers we have.

INTERNAL TRIGGERS

Anger: A feeling of keen displeasure. Usually with a desire to punish for what we regard as wrong towards ourselves or others.

Anxiety: A multisystem response to a perceived threat or danger. As far as we know, anxiety is a uniquely human experience.

Feeling Abandoned: To give up, sometimes completely or forever.

Feeling out of Control: No longer under management, direction or regulation. Not manageable, unruly.

Feeling Lonely: Having a feeling of depression or sadness, lonesome.

Feeling Vulnerable: Capable of being emotionally wounded or hurt and open to temptation.

Frustration: the condition that results when an impulse or an action is thwarted by an external or internal force.

Muscle Tension: Typically caused by the effects of stress and can lead to episodes of back pain.

Pain: An unpleasant sensation occurring in varying degrees as a consequence of an emotional disorder.

Racing Heart Beat: Palpitations are heartbeat sensations that feet like pounding or racing.

Sadness: Characterized by emotions ranging from mild discontentment to deep grief.

EXTERNAL TRIGGERS
➤ A specific place that brings up bad memories
➤ Arguing
➤ Anniversaries
➤ Certain Smells
➤ Holidays
➤ News that bring up traumatic events
➤ Seeing a bad car accident
➤ Watching a movie or television show that reminds you of a traumatic event or situation

Physical Health Problems caused by PTSD
The Veterans Administration has done studies and found that people with PTSD are more likely to experience more physical and health problems then people without it. Here are a few examples:
Arthritis
Diabetes
Heart related problems
Digestive problems
Reproductive system problems
Respiratory system problems
PTSD related physical health problems will seek health care more that people without it. Studies have found that PTSD is unique in its own way, as opposed to simply being exposed to a traumatic event which puts people at risk for developing physical health problems. PTSD puts an emotional strain and stress and tremendous physical struggles on a person.

I used to engage in risky and unsafe behavior like alcohol and drug use. My symptoms put me in a constant state of anxiety and stress. These combined symptoms put a tremendous strain and stress on my body and mind. Hopefully, they have not yet caused any health problems or illness.

Finding a Source
Please note this information: it is vital to all military personnel to maintain a source for help with PTSD. The information tells of the

correct way to receive help and file claims. Do not be afraid to ask for help. Make sure that your material is documented with time and dates. You have the right to protect yourself and your family.

The following is a list of help lines:

Air Force Palace HART
1-800-774-1361
E-Mail: severelyinjured@militaryonesource.com

American Love and Appreciation Fund
1-305-673-2856

Army Wounded Warrior Program
1-800-237-1336 or 1-800-833-6622

Department of Human Services & Deployment
1-800-497-6261

Marine for Life
1-866-645-8762
E-mail: injuredsupport@M4L.usmc.mil

Military Source One
1-800-342-9647

Military Severely Injured Center
1-800-774-1361

National Coalition Against Sexual Assault
1-717-728-9764

National Alliance for Mentally Ill
1-800-950-6264

Mental Health Association
1-800– 969-6642

Navy Safe Harbor
1-800-774-1361

Operation Comfort (Veterans & Families)
1-866-632-7876 or 1-866 NEAR TO U

PTSD Sanctuary
1-800-THERAPIST

PTSD Information Hotline
1-802-296-6300

PFC Curtis Butler III in Baghdad

IN CONCLUSION

I pray that politicians and physicians learn more about Post Traumatic Stress Disorder from Soldiers coming back from the War Zone. PTSD is a disease like cancer eating away at us day by day. Doctors say that the PTSD does not make you kill. Let me remind you of the Sergeant that killed those five soldiers at Camp Liberty where President Obama recently visited. Soon you will be reading more stories like the one you just read about me. PTSD has ingrained problems that can trigger killing instincts like seeing or hearing your battle buddies get killed or injured.

Flashbacks, intrusive emotions, bad memories, nightmares and night terrors, explosive outbursts, irritability and panic symptoms are common. Congressional Representatives should go on missions with the soldiers and live on the FOB for a couple of months. Go to the hospitals and see the soldiers that by the grace of God have survived an IED attack, rocket attack or a gun battle. If the soldiers keep getting denied their benefits by the VA, you need not worry about the gangs, you need to worry about the soldiers begging for assistance that can lead to a lot of time bombs going off in your city. Please help.

My name is Curtis Butler III. I hope that you have enjoyed this book that I have written while studying for my degree in business and accounting at the University of Phoenix. In this book I write about things that happened to me in life. The good things and bad, the bias during my summary court martial, the lies and misrepresentations of my unit from the top of the chain of command. Soldiers calling me out on the blog. Writing about the problems I see at the VA, post traumatic stress disorder as the government sees it. The Veterans from past wars to the future soldiers fighting for freedom, but cannot receive proper treatment and their disability credits they all deserve. It's time for a change.

The Author

PHOTO GALERY

Eagle standing proud
and a great flag

SPC Curtis Butler III Culinary award and Coins for
Best Turkey Display, 2005 Hanau, Germany.

SPC Curtis Butler III and SSG Gabriel Pedroza
Cooking a pig 2005 Hanau, Germany

SPC Curtis Butler III Culinary Award and coins for best
turkey and ham display 2005 at Hanau, Germany

Curtis Butler enjoying a Mets baseball game in 2005 at Queens, NY

Shea Stadium in Queens New York - Go Mets!

Battery Park in
Charleston, SC

Aunt Gloria (top left), Aunt Rose (l) and Aunt Sam (r)

Patricia (l), Curtis (c) and Rudy (r) from El Zarape Restaurant

Curtis & Michelle

Curtis & Pam from SportsCards.com

Grandparents Curtis Butler Sr. and Justine Washington Butler

Curtis Butler III

Uncle Col Anthony Spencer (Ret) [l], SSG Curtis
Butler Jr. (Ret) [m] and Aunt Jeanette [r]

Directions to the airport in Baghdad

CPSIA information can be obtained at www.ICGtesting.com
Printed in the USA
LVOW051745181212

312260LV00006B/774/P